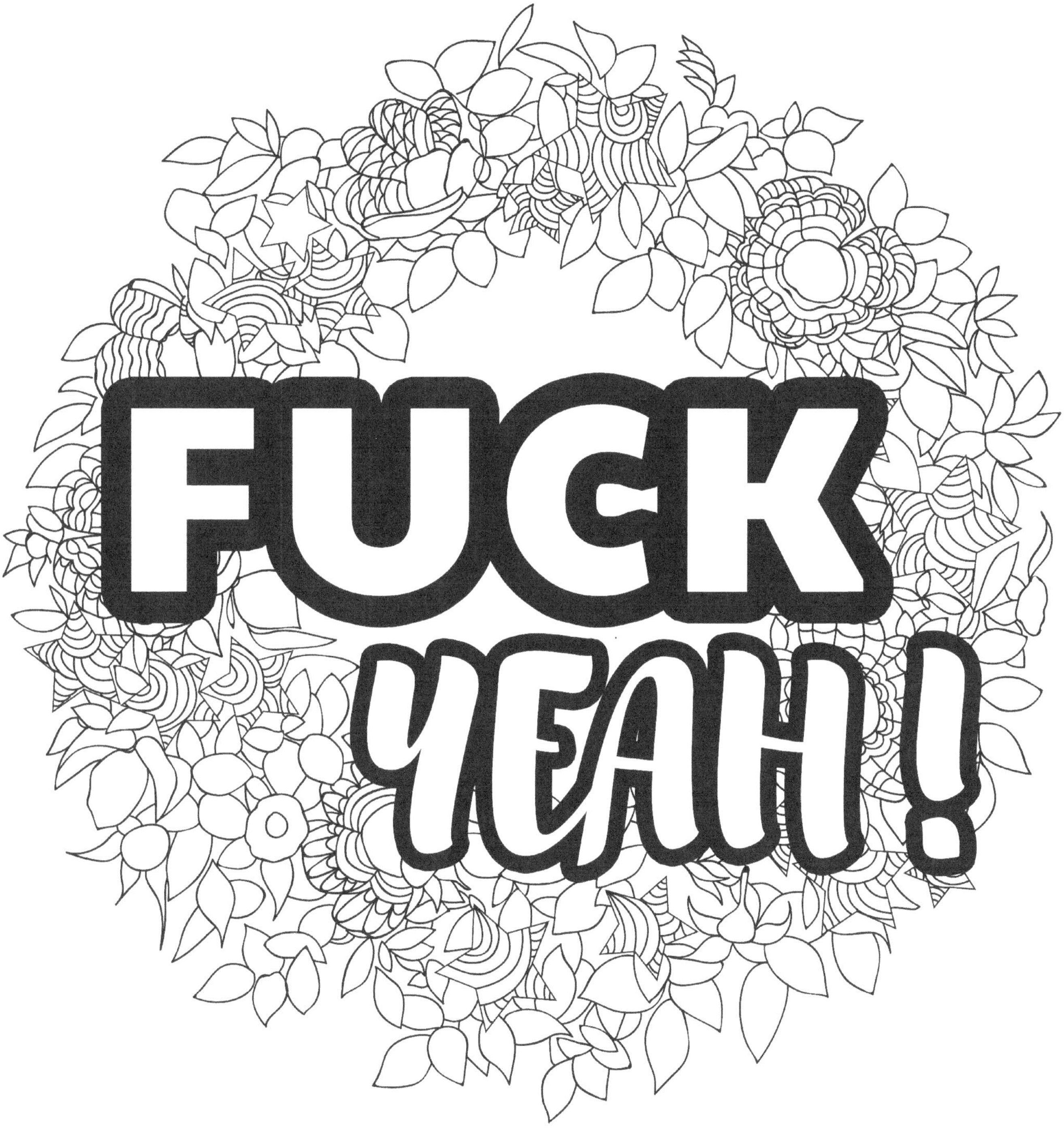
FUCK
YEAH!

Illustrated by:
Mandala & Caricature Illustration
Joshua Lazana Lagman and Jade Villaremo

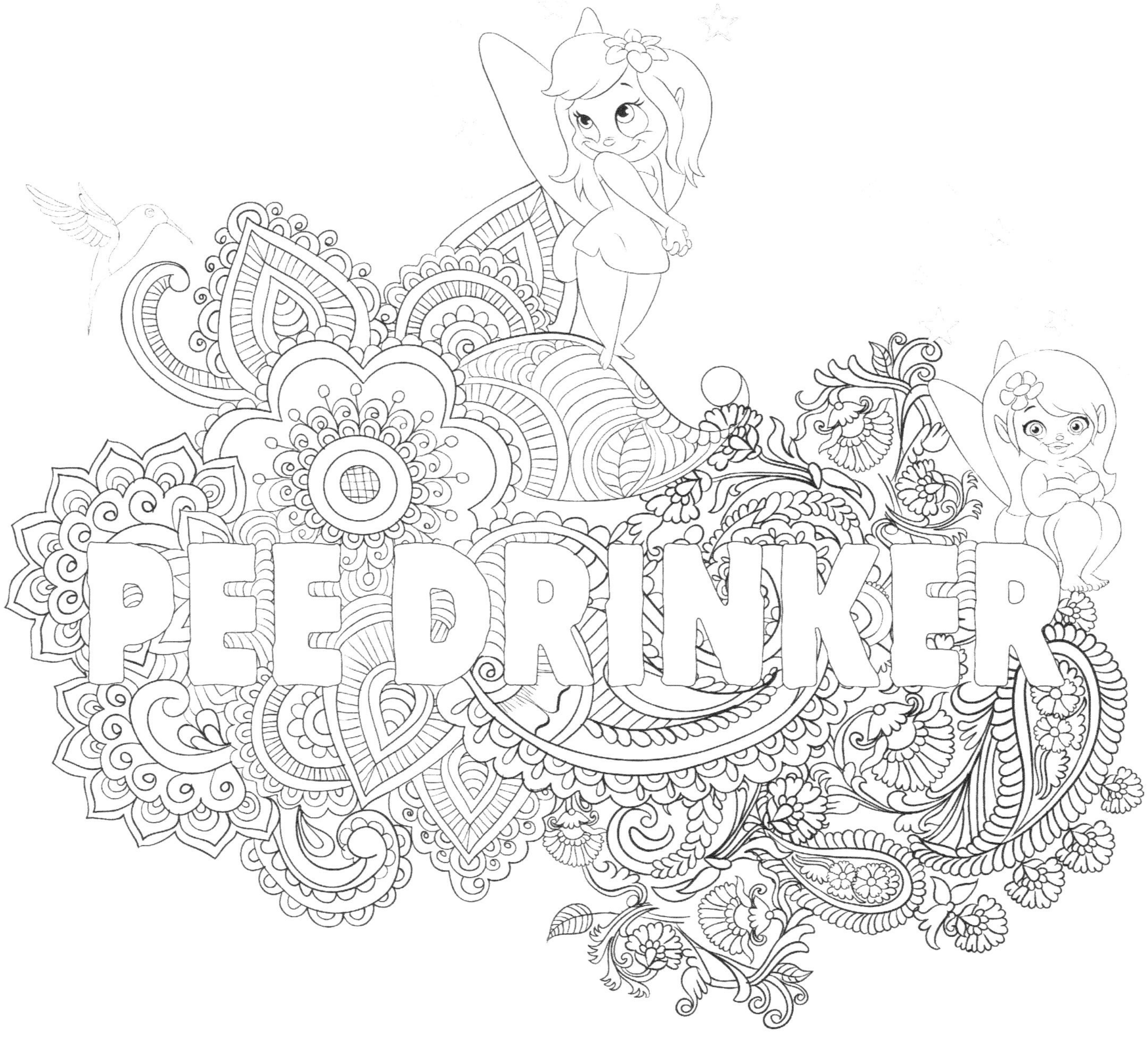
PEE DRINKER

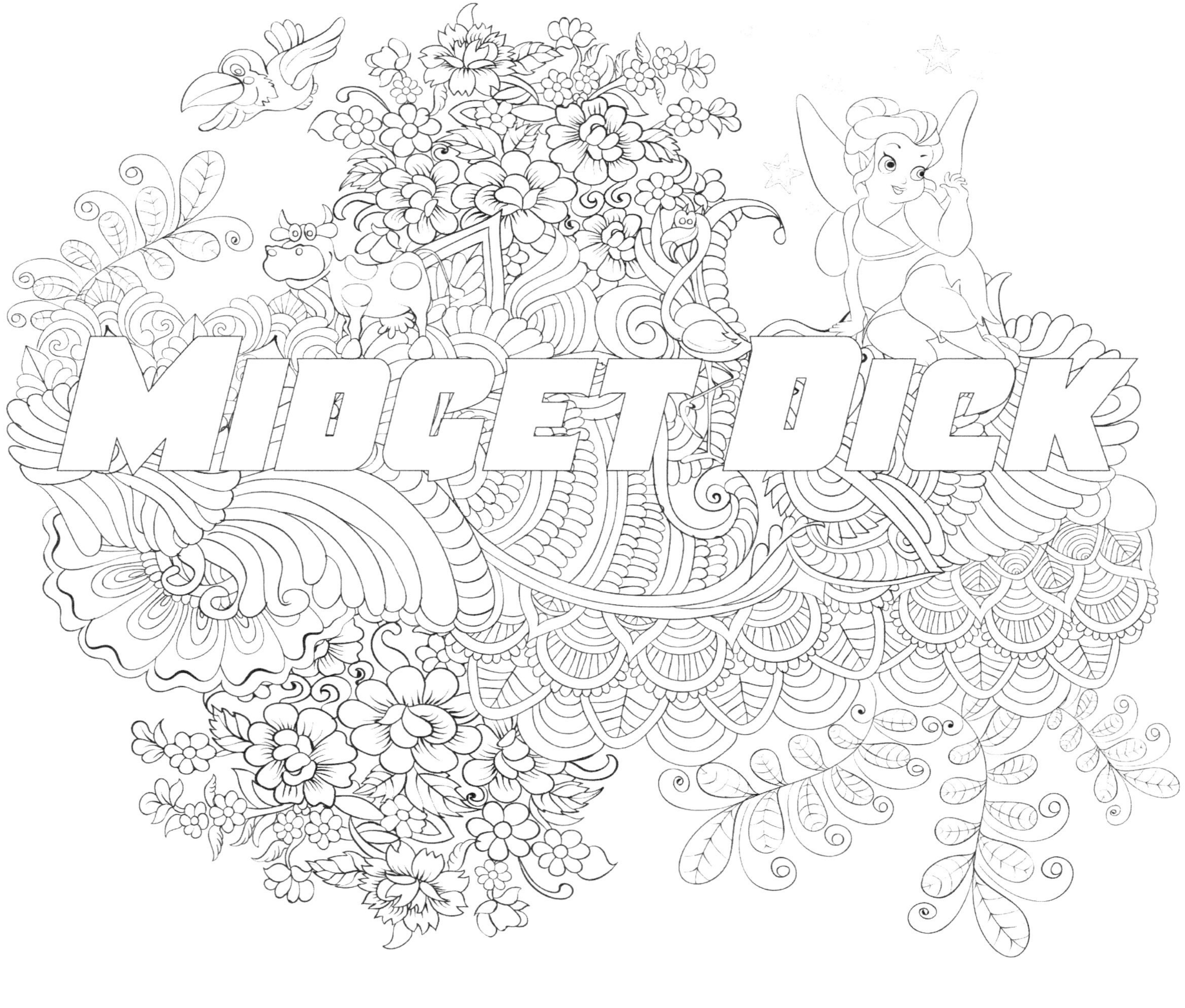
MIDGET DICK

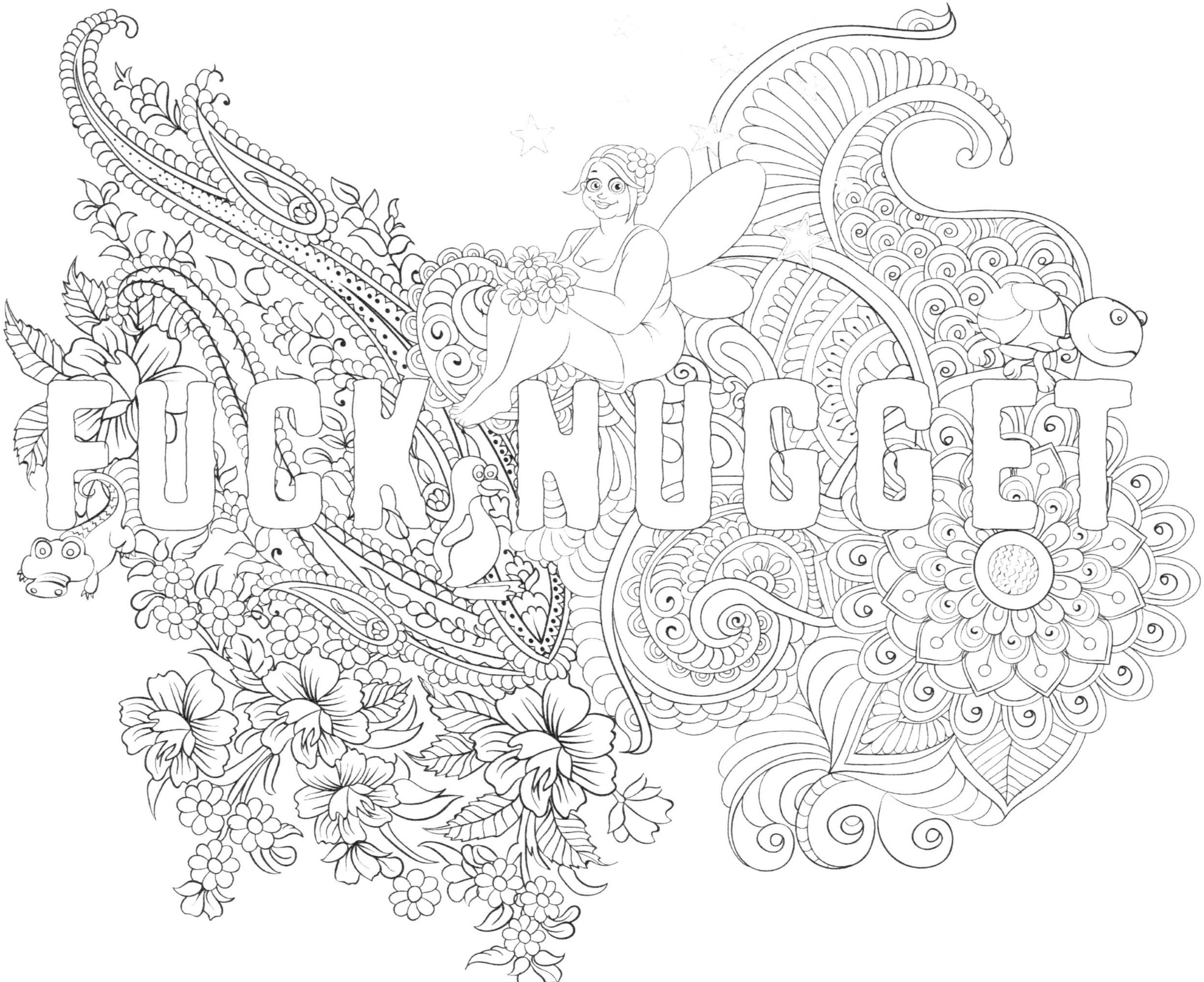
FUCKNUGGET

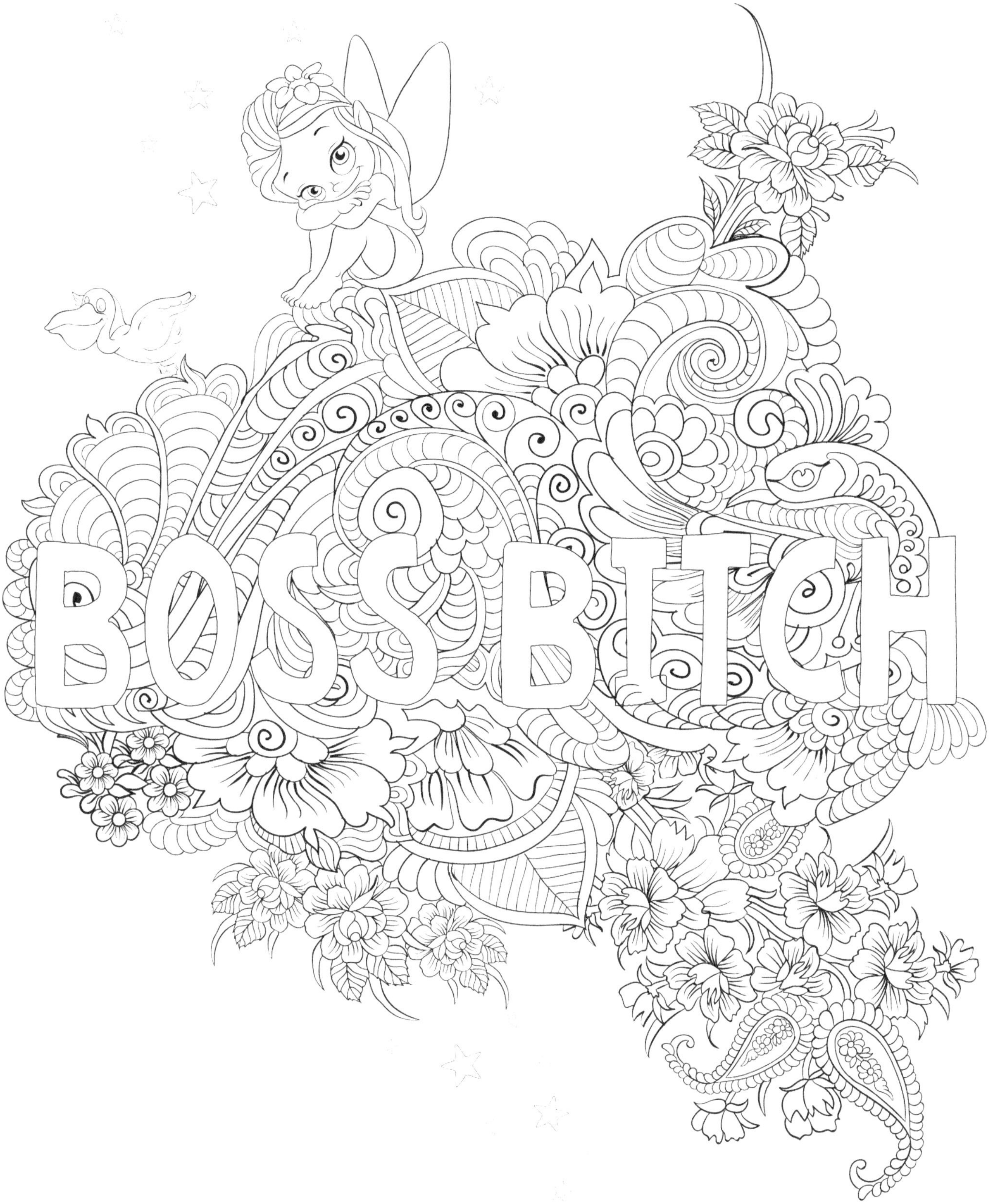
BOSS BITCH

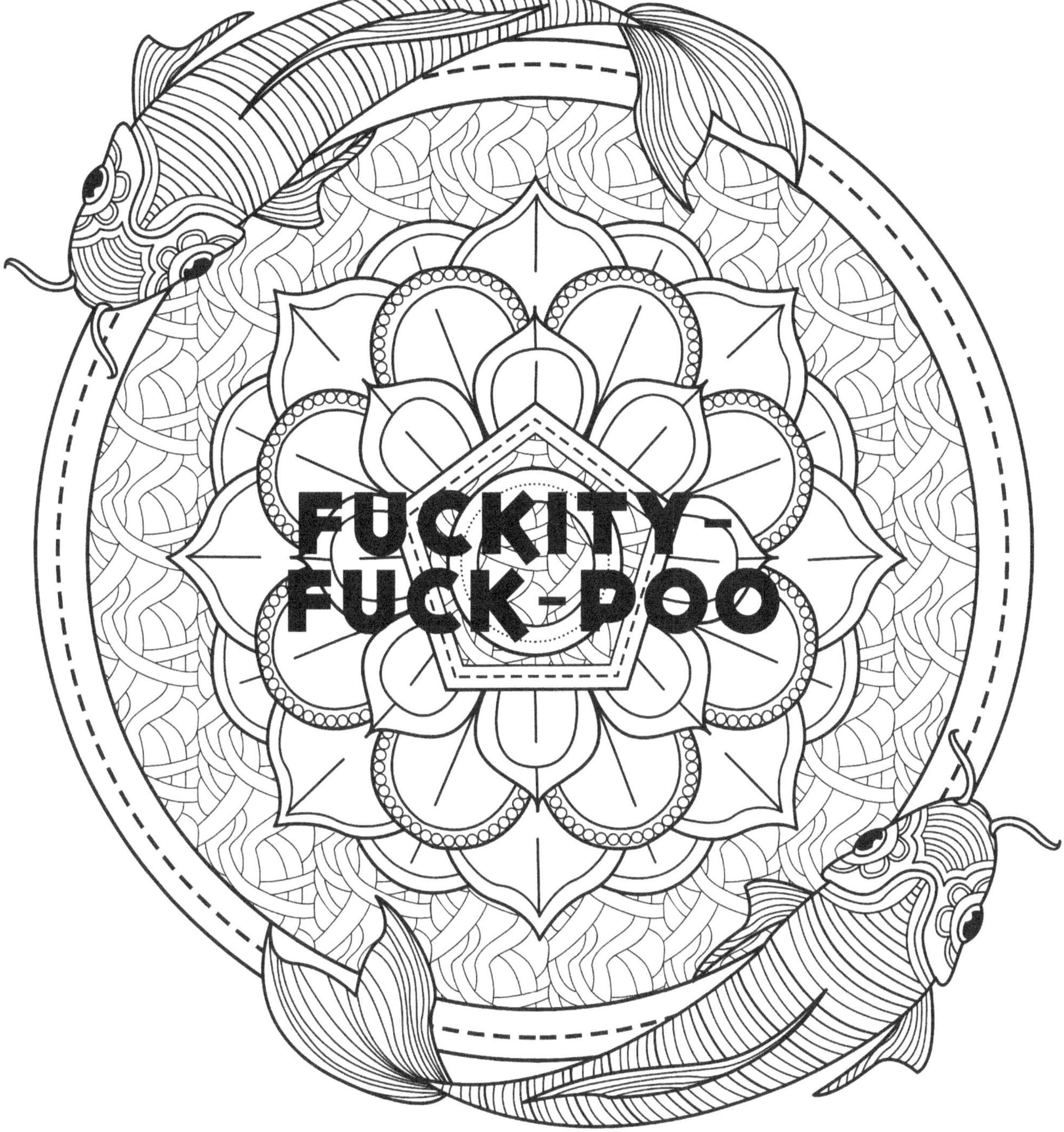
FUCKITY-
FUCK-POO

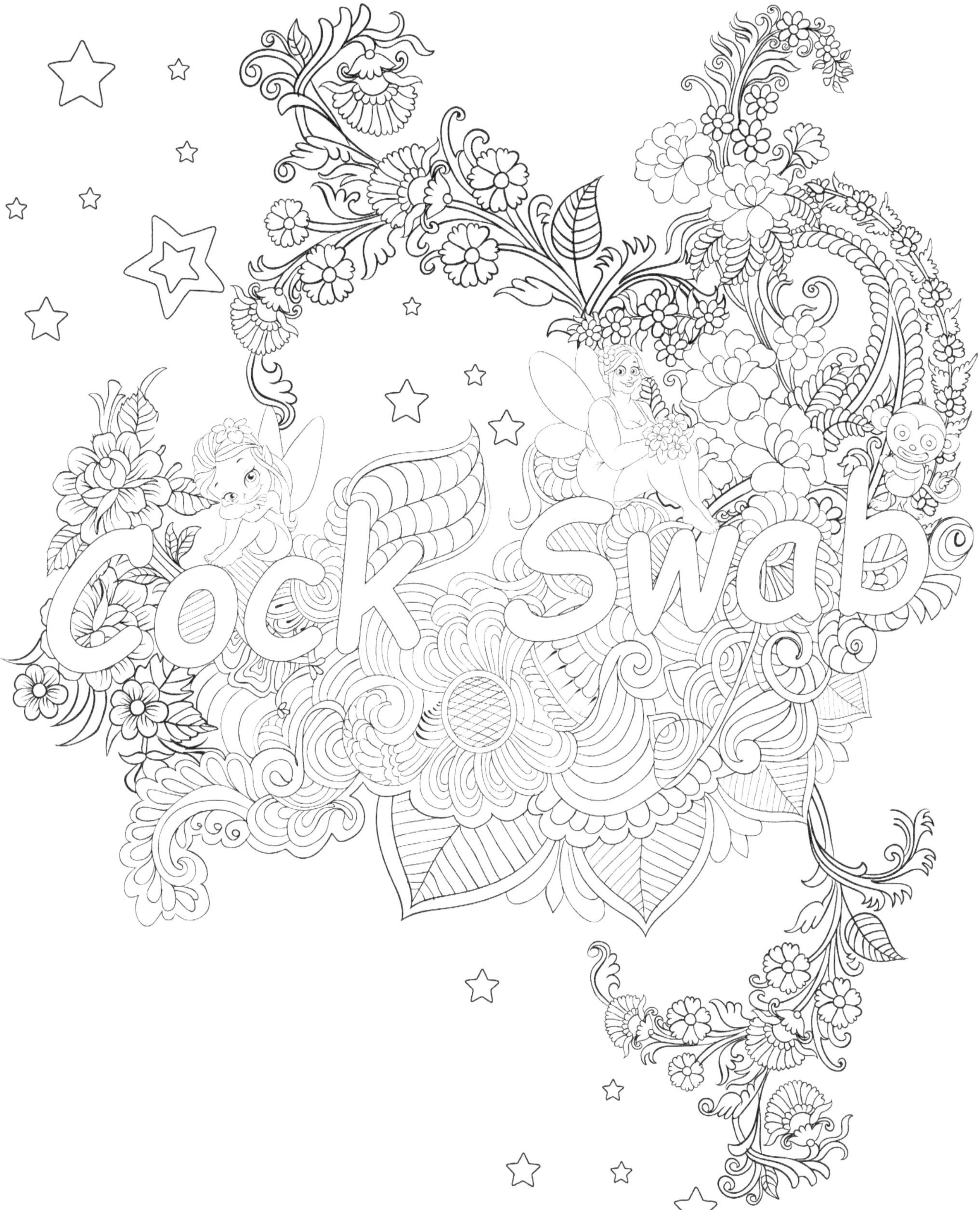
Cock Swab

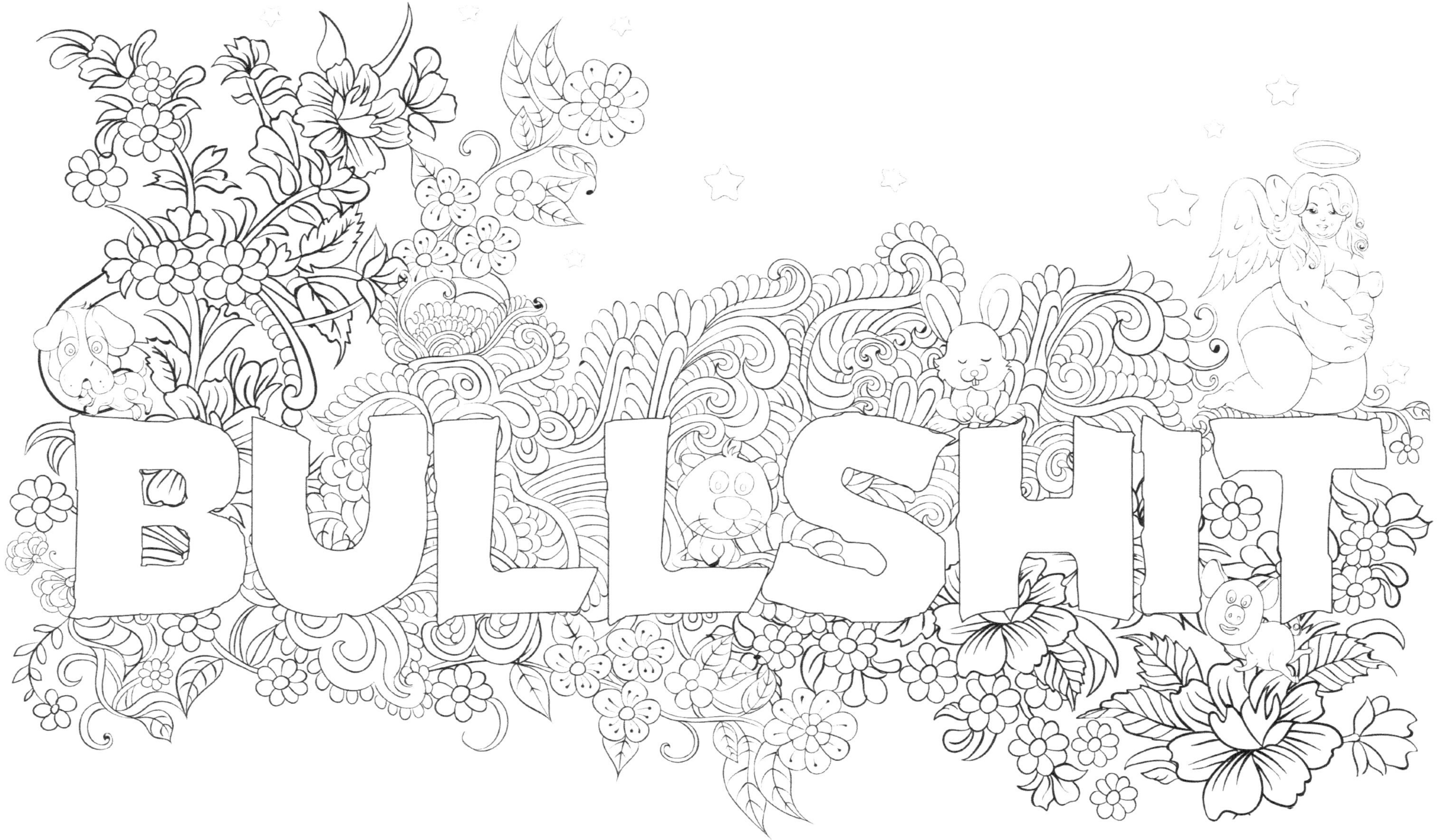
BULLSHIT

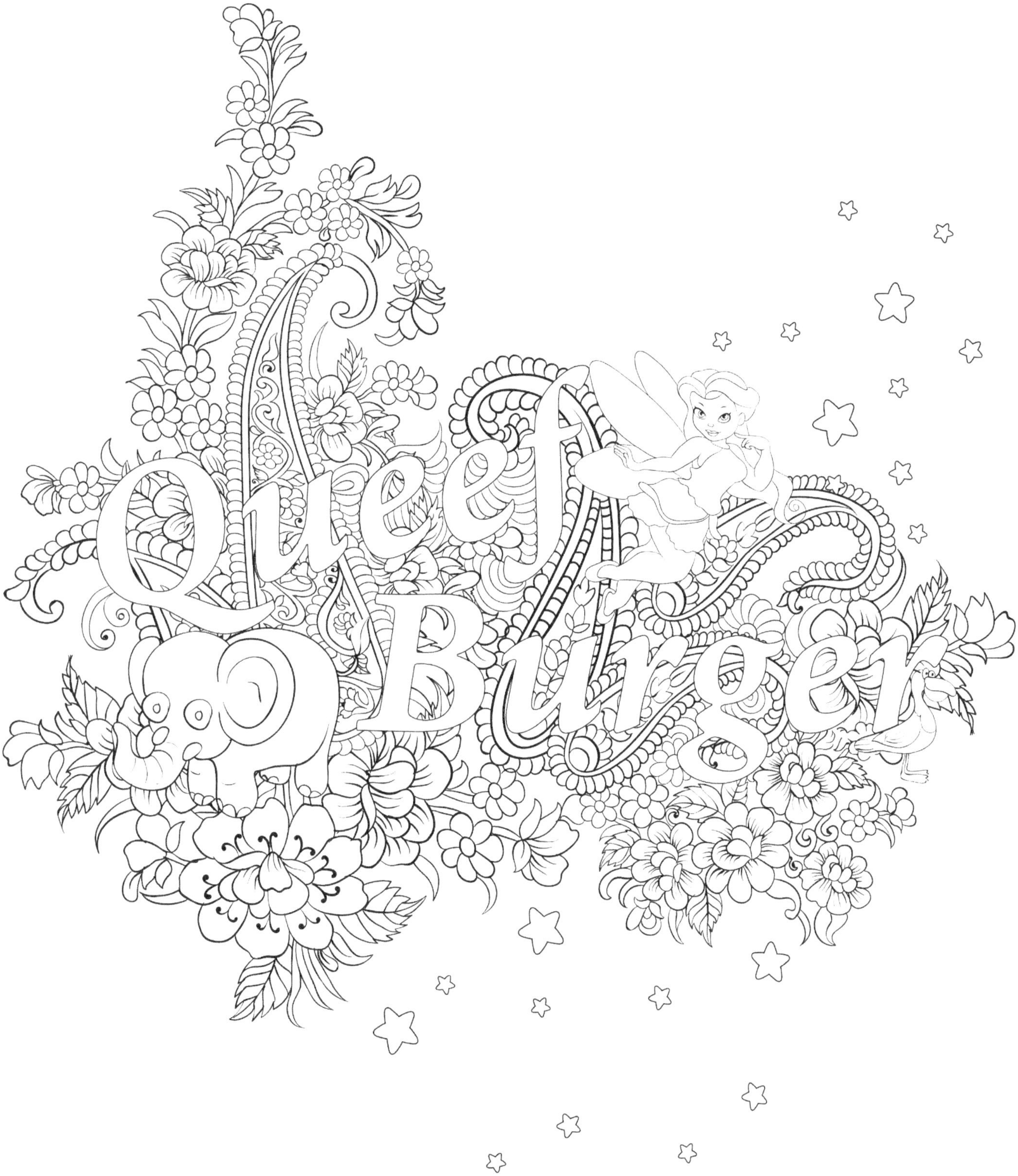
Queef
Burger

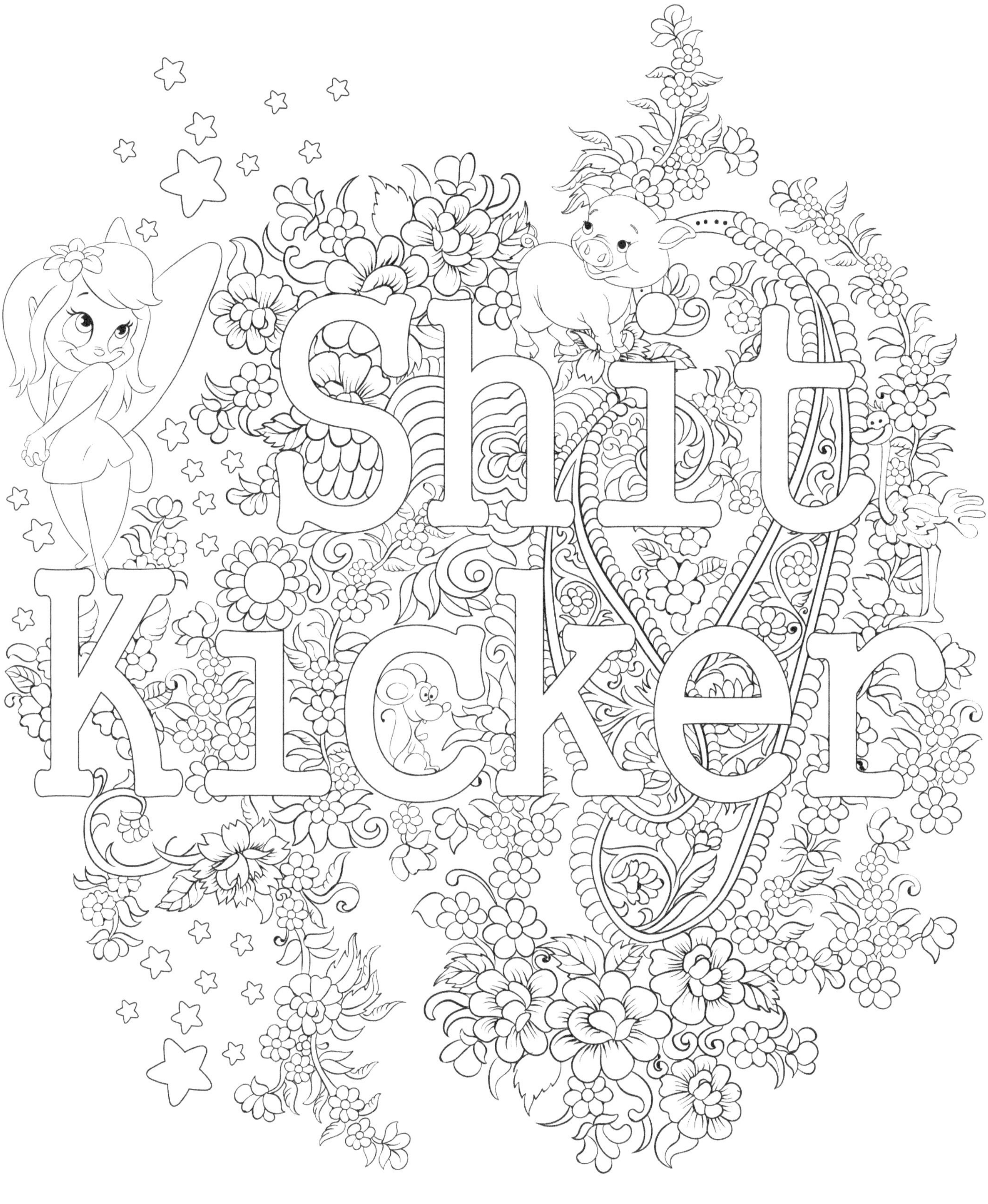
Shit
Kicker

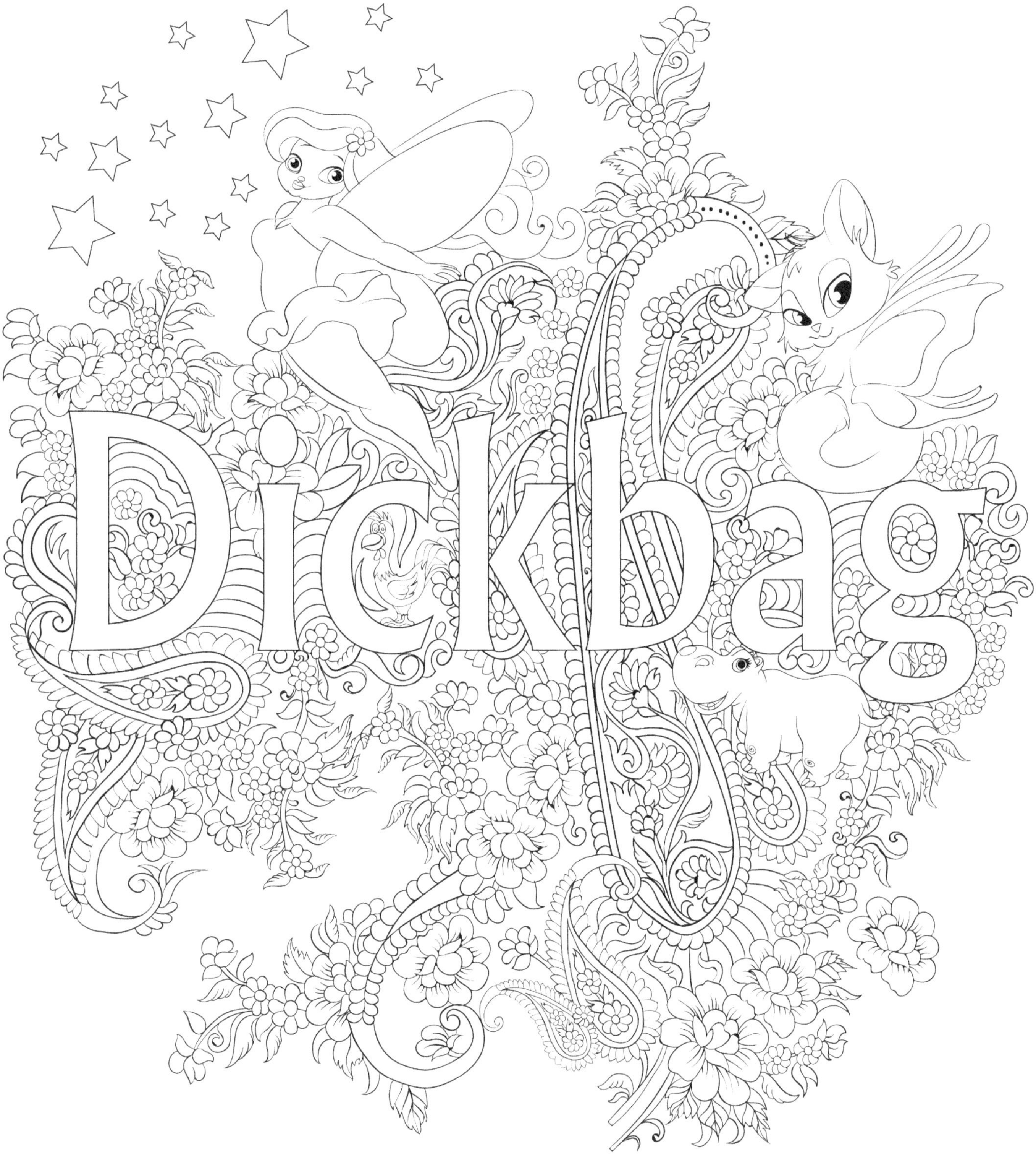
Dickbag

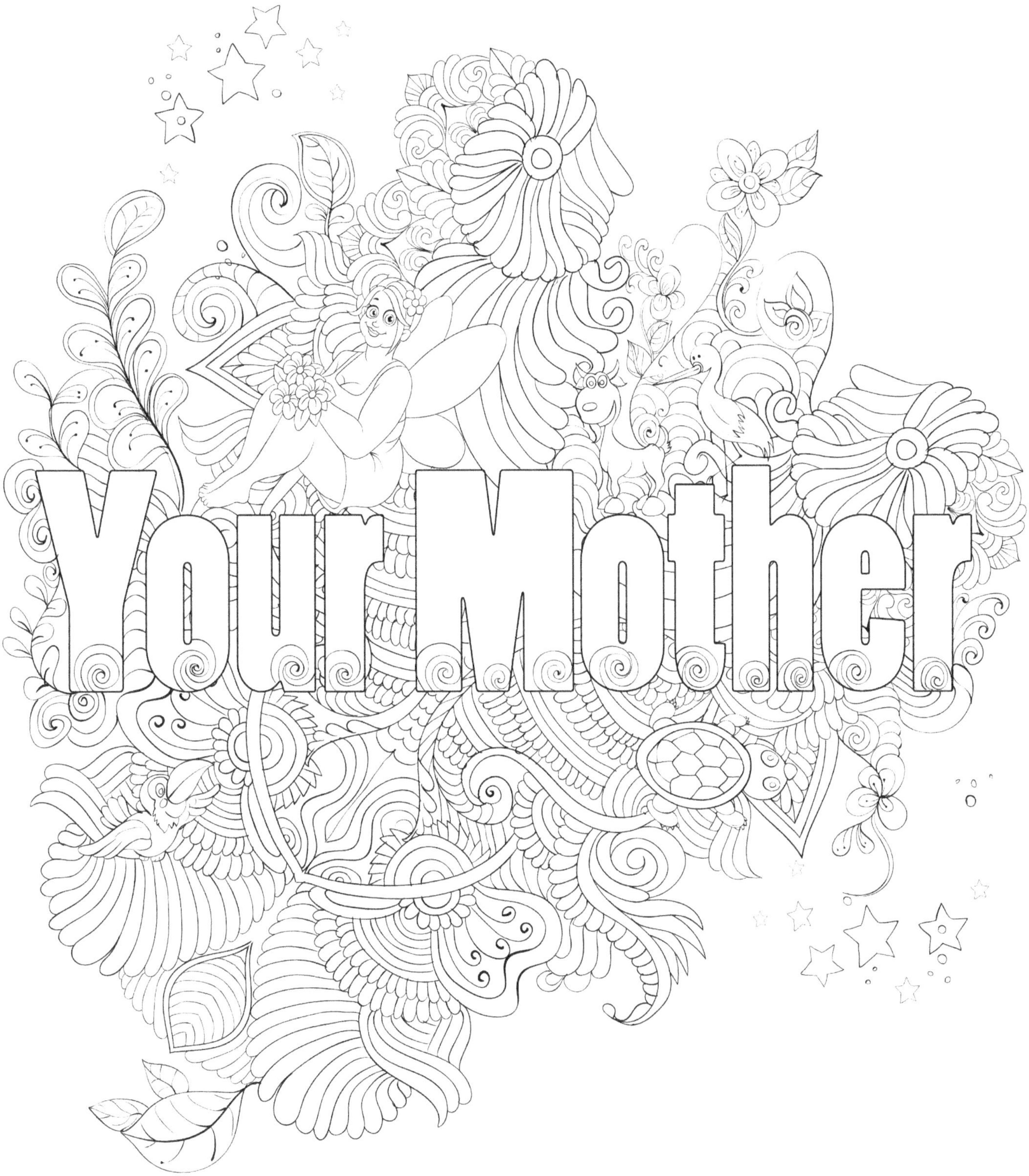
Your Mother

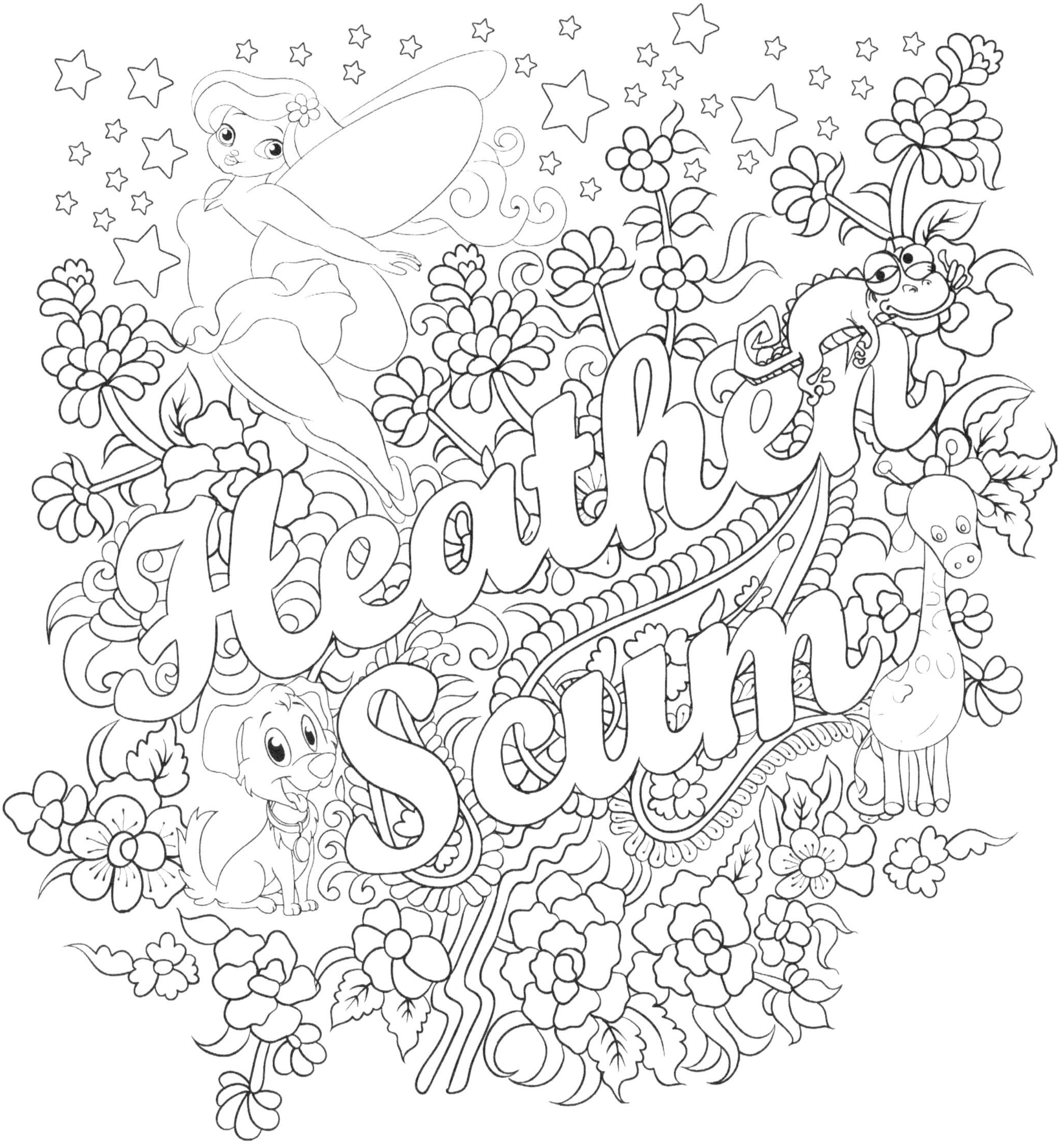
Heather
Scum

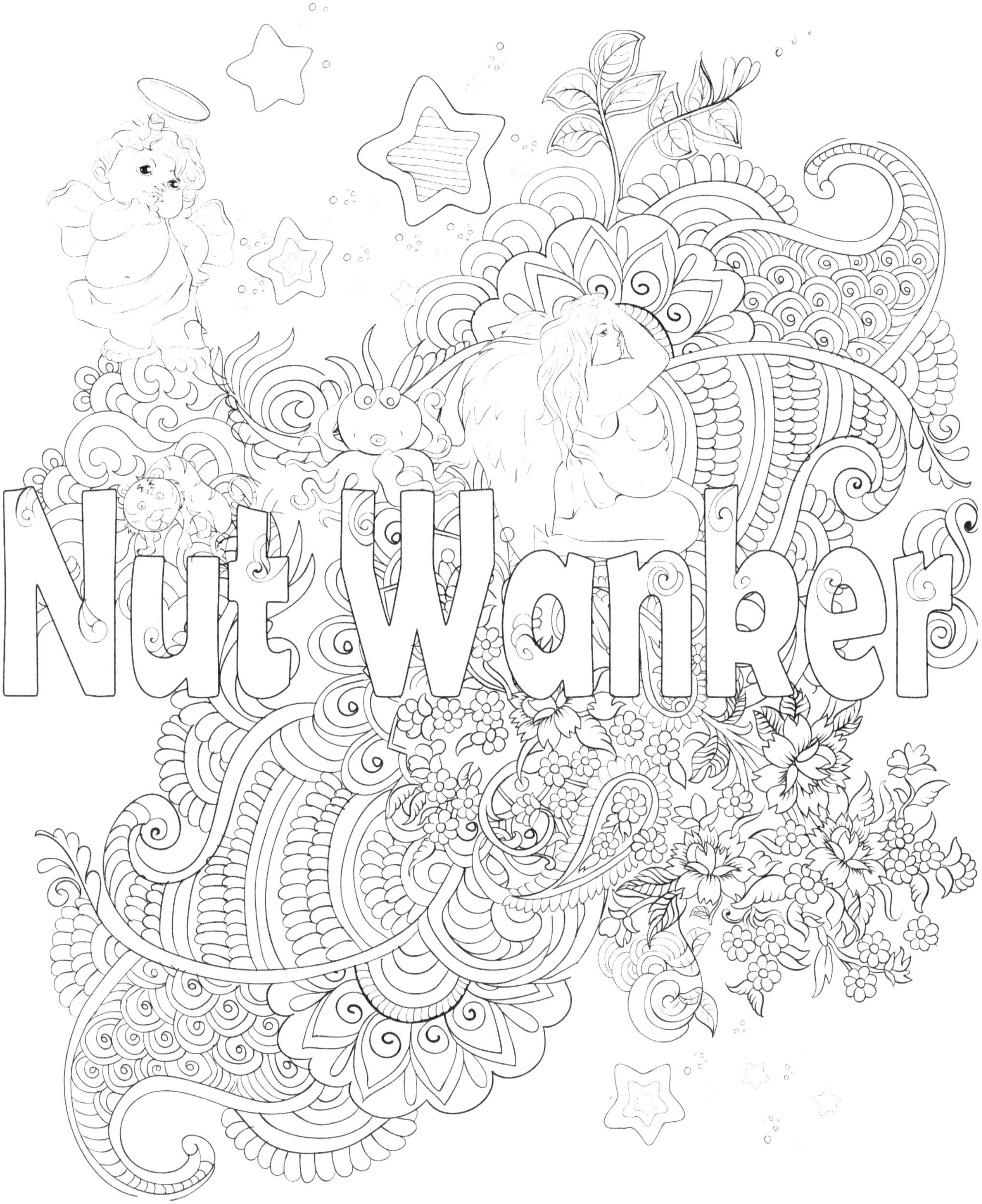
Nut Wanker

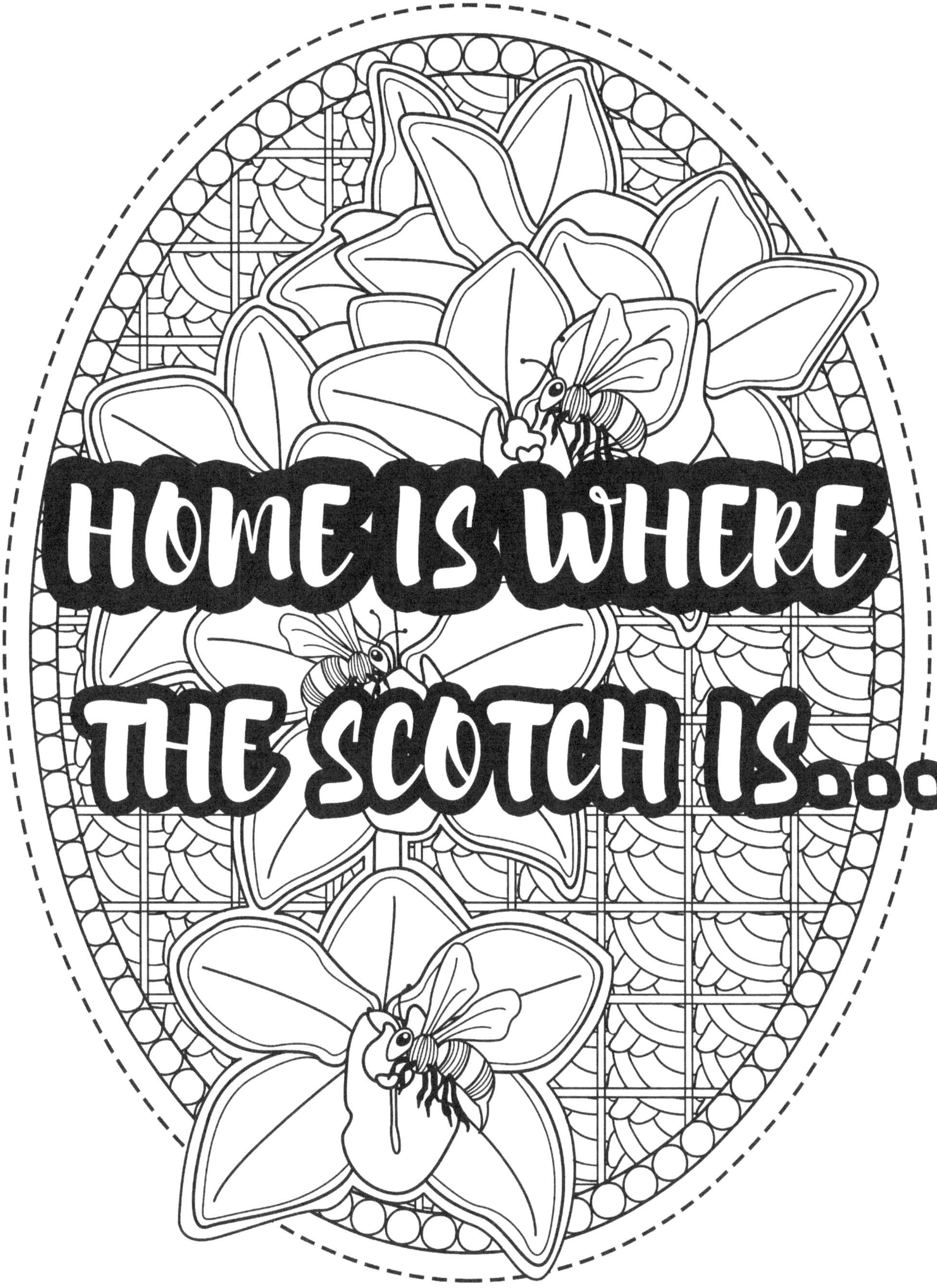
HOME IS WHERE
THE SCOTCH IS...

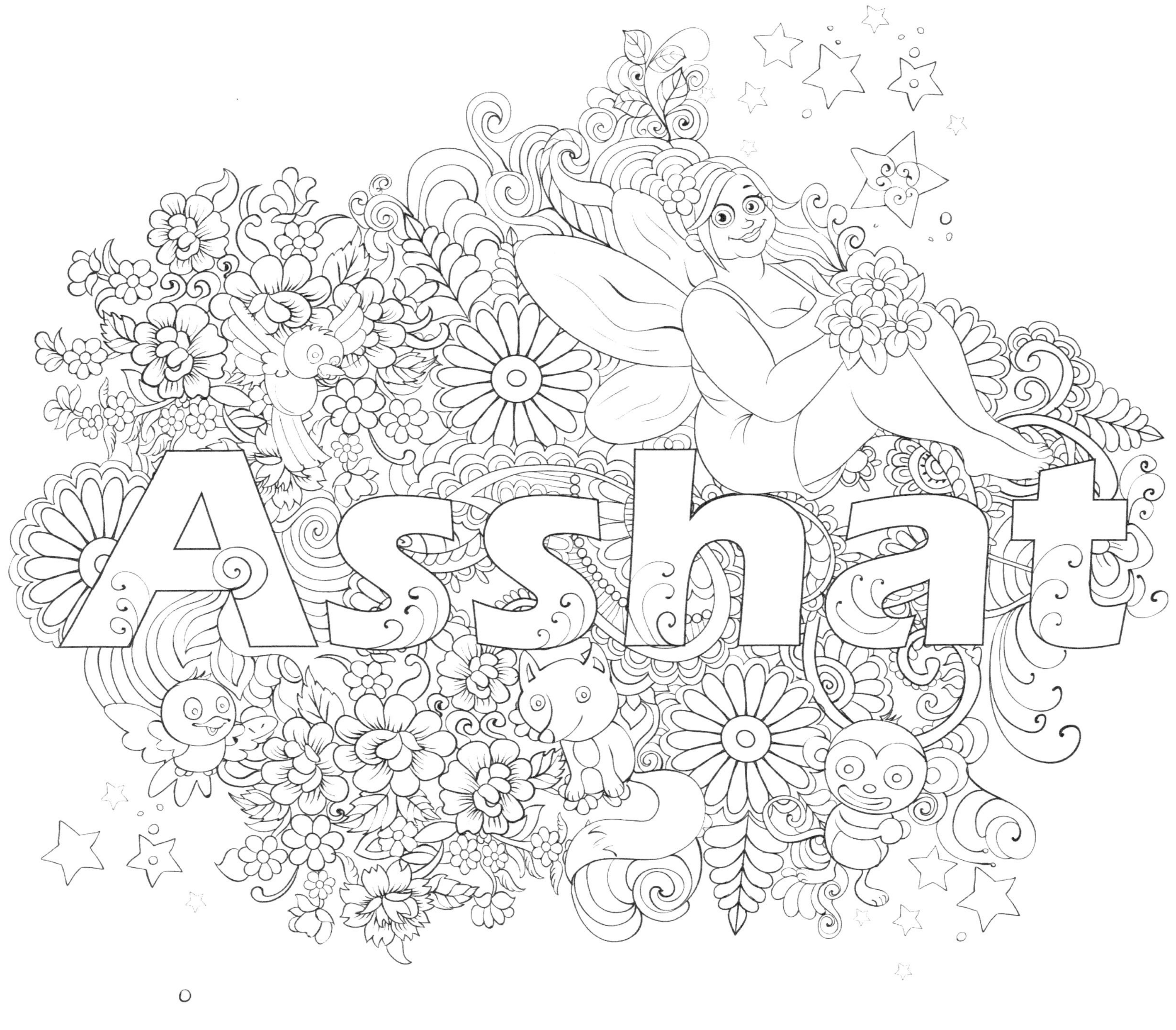
Asshat

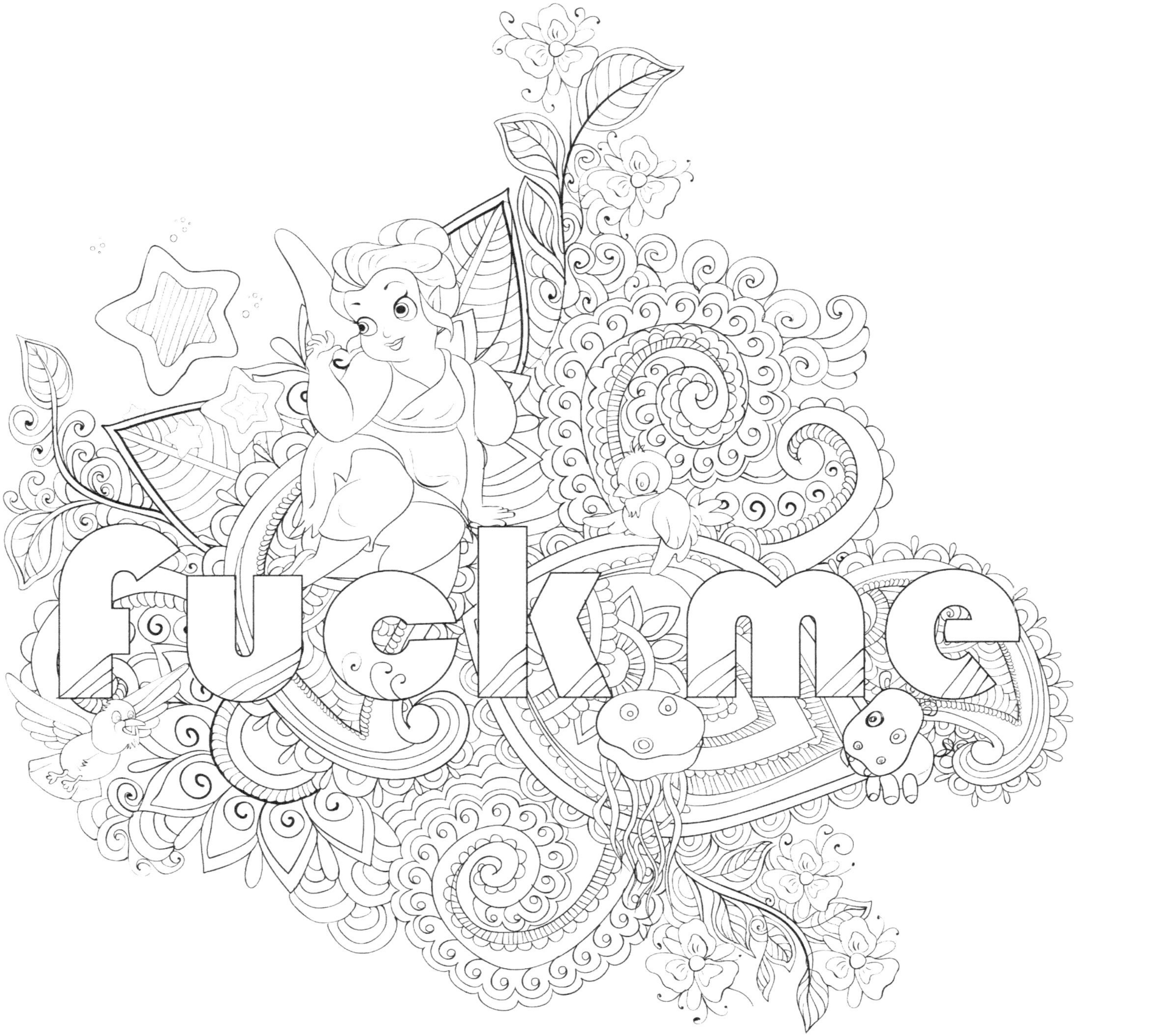
Fuck me

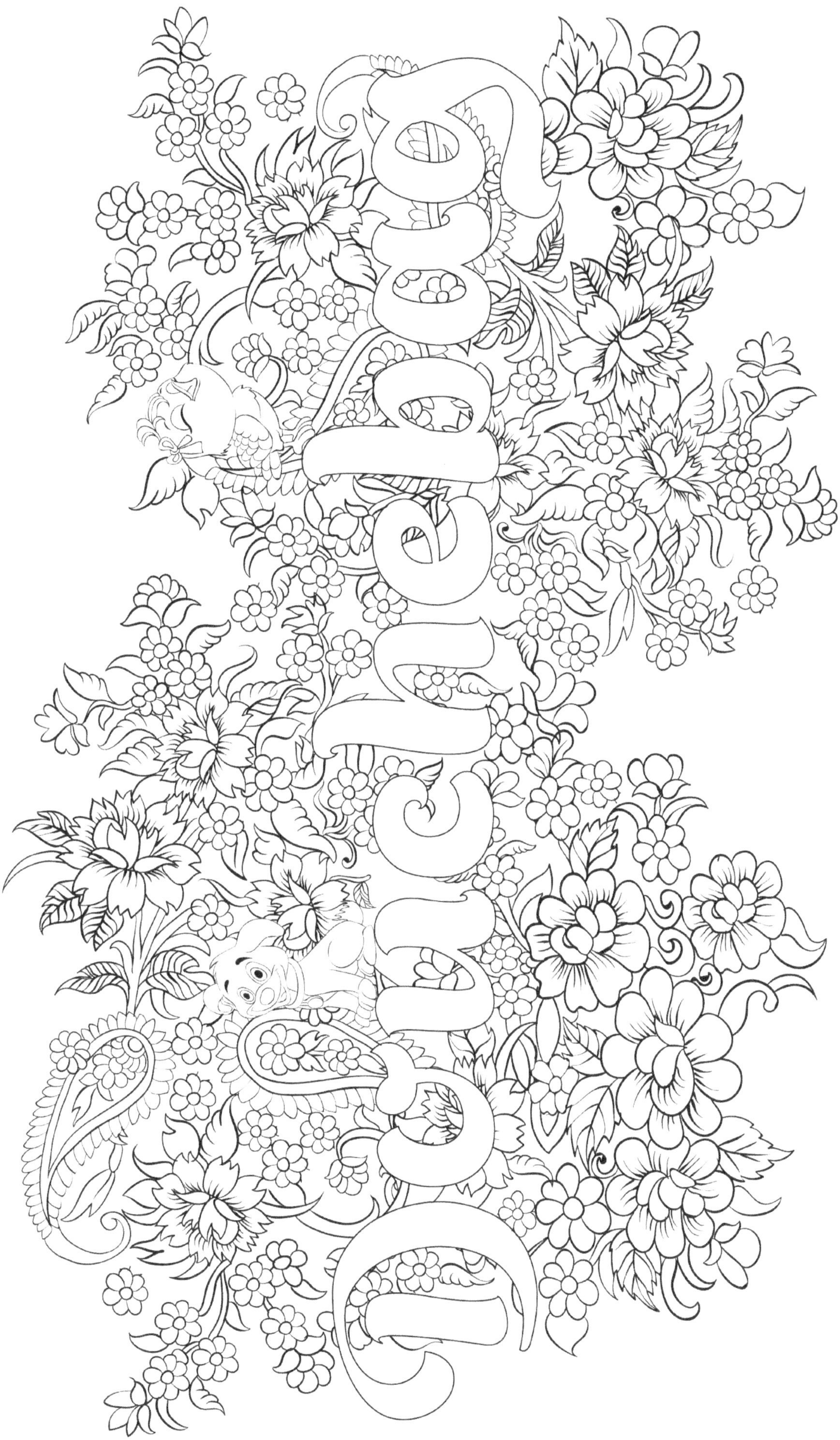
Douchebag

PIECE OF GARBAGE

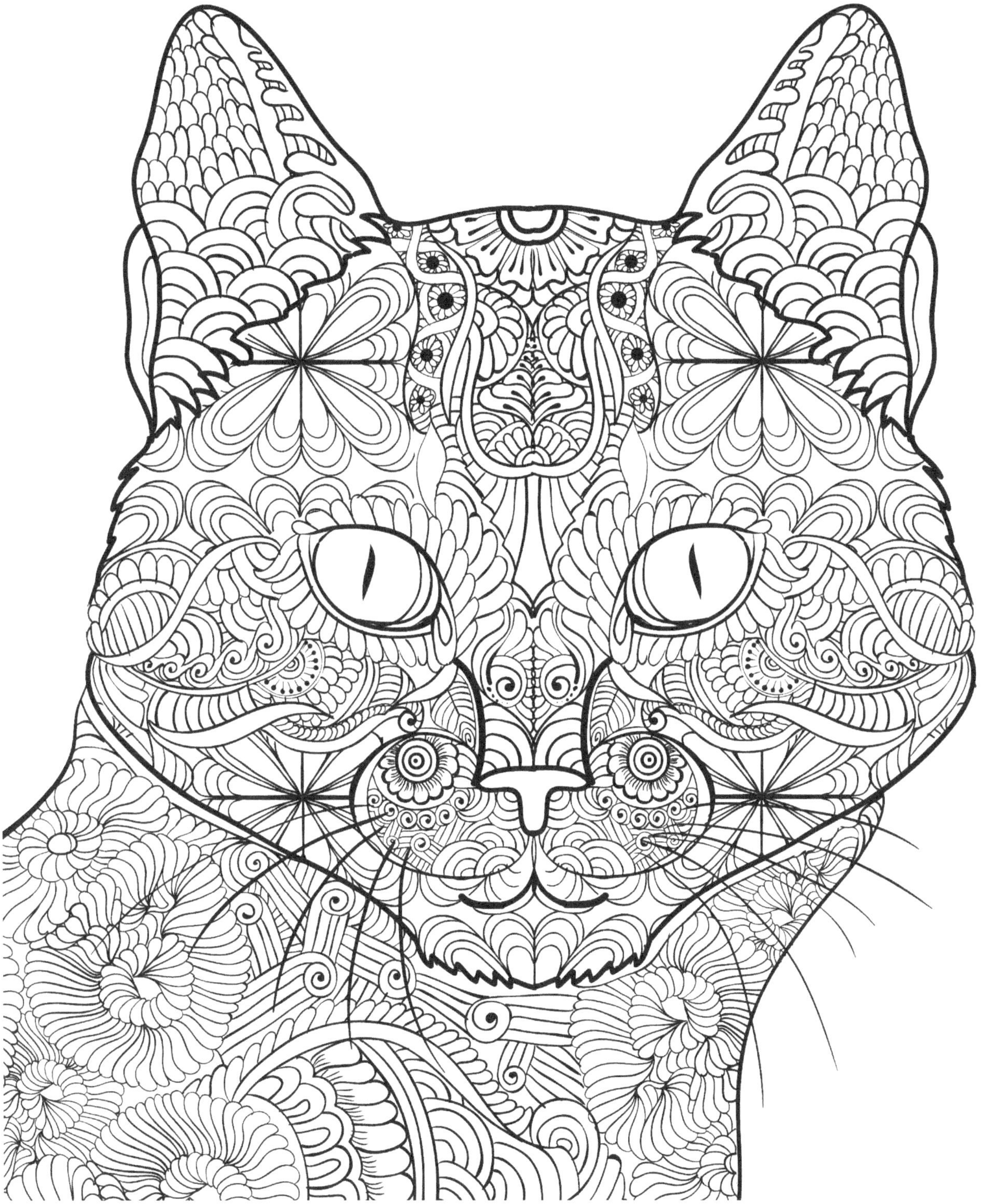

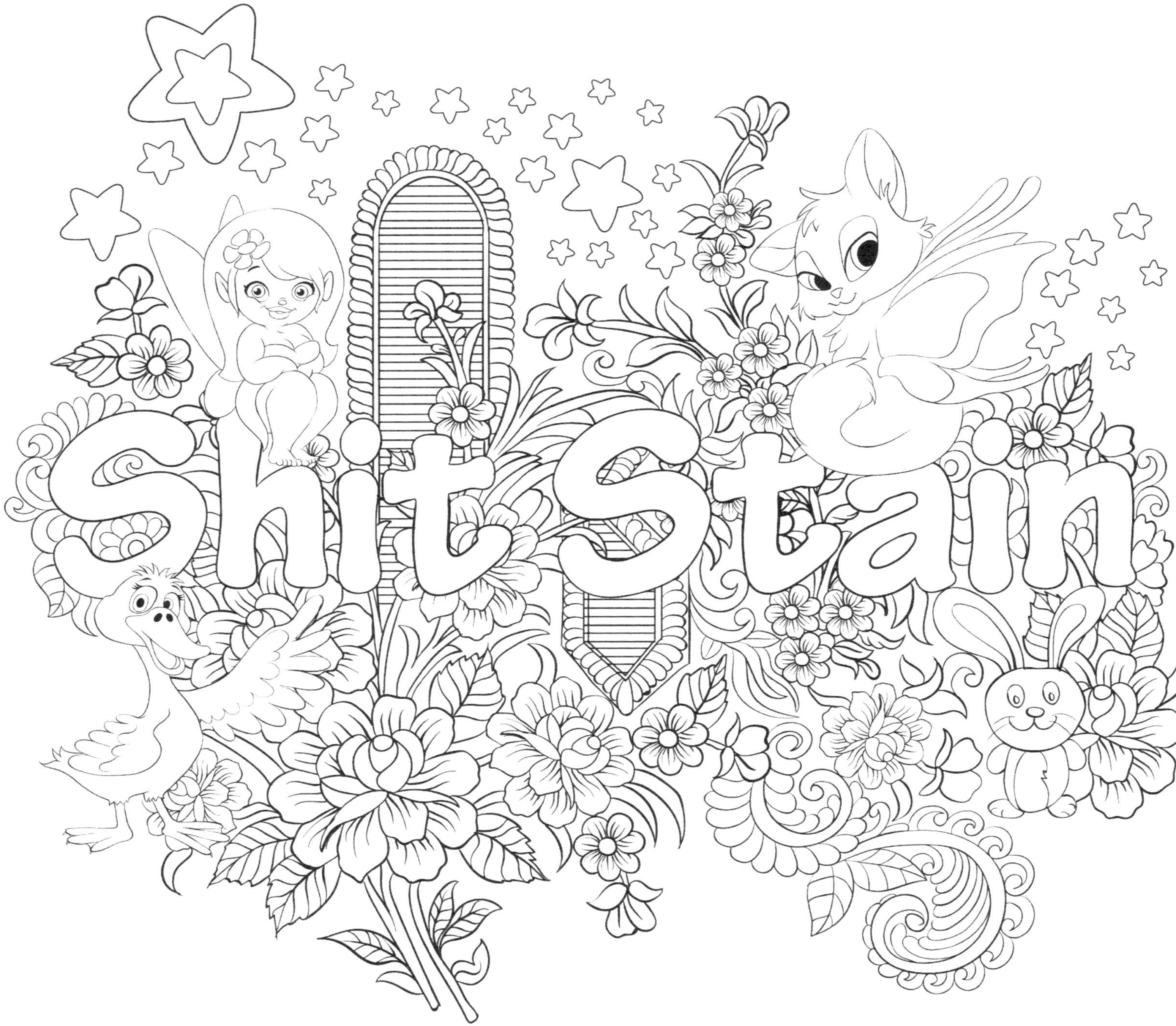
Shit Stain

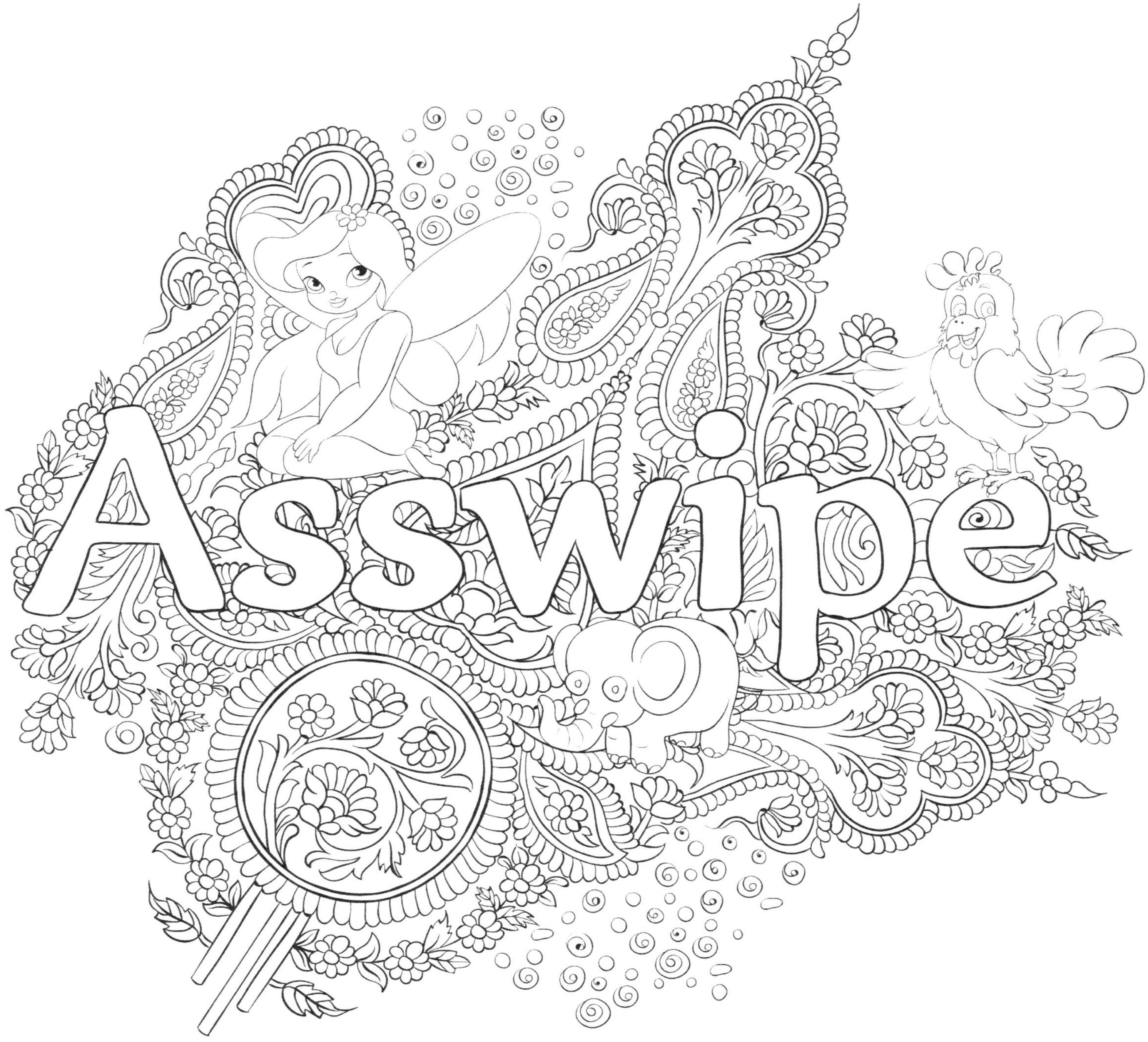
Asswipe

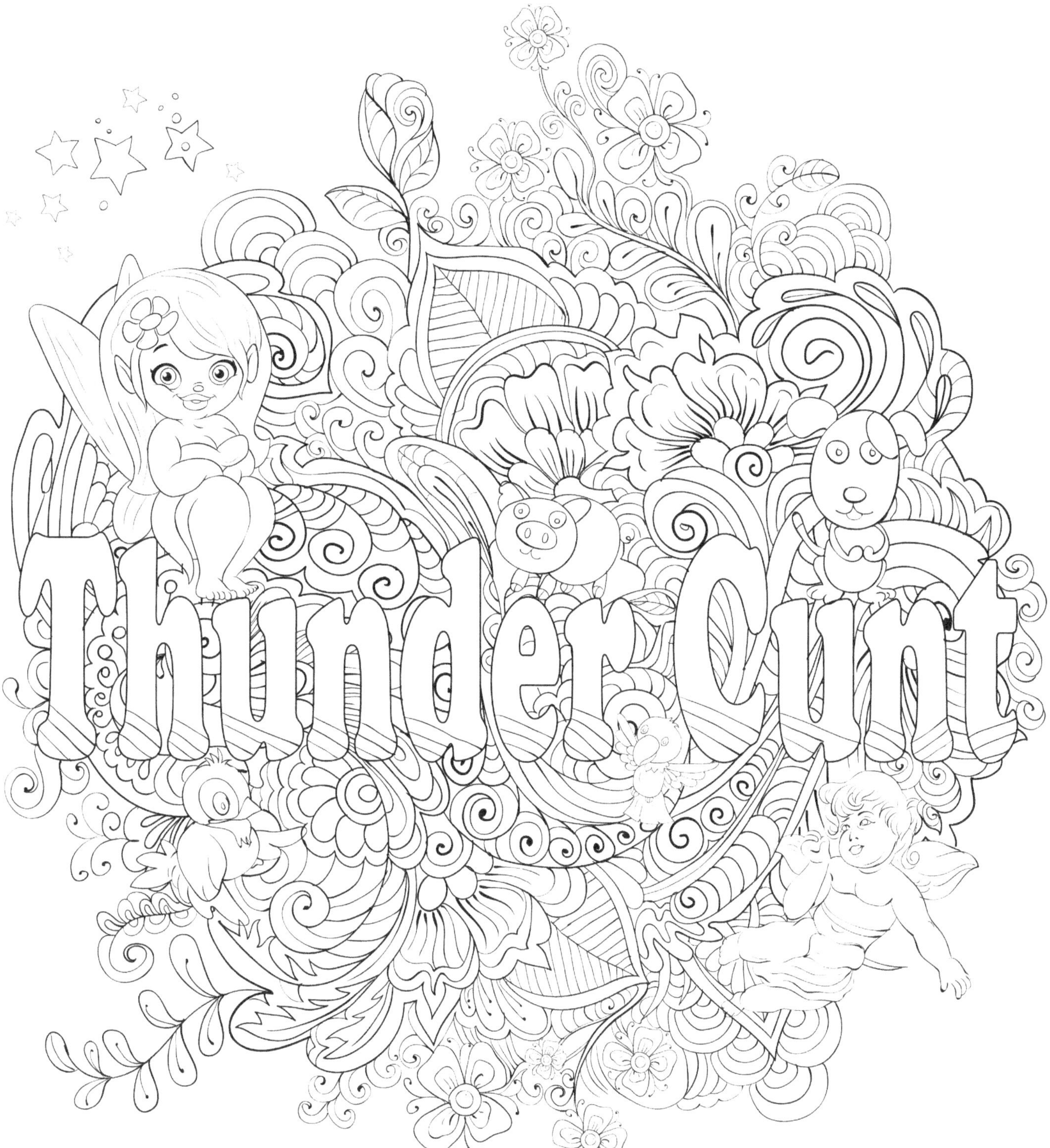
Thunder Cunt

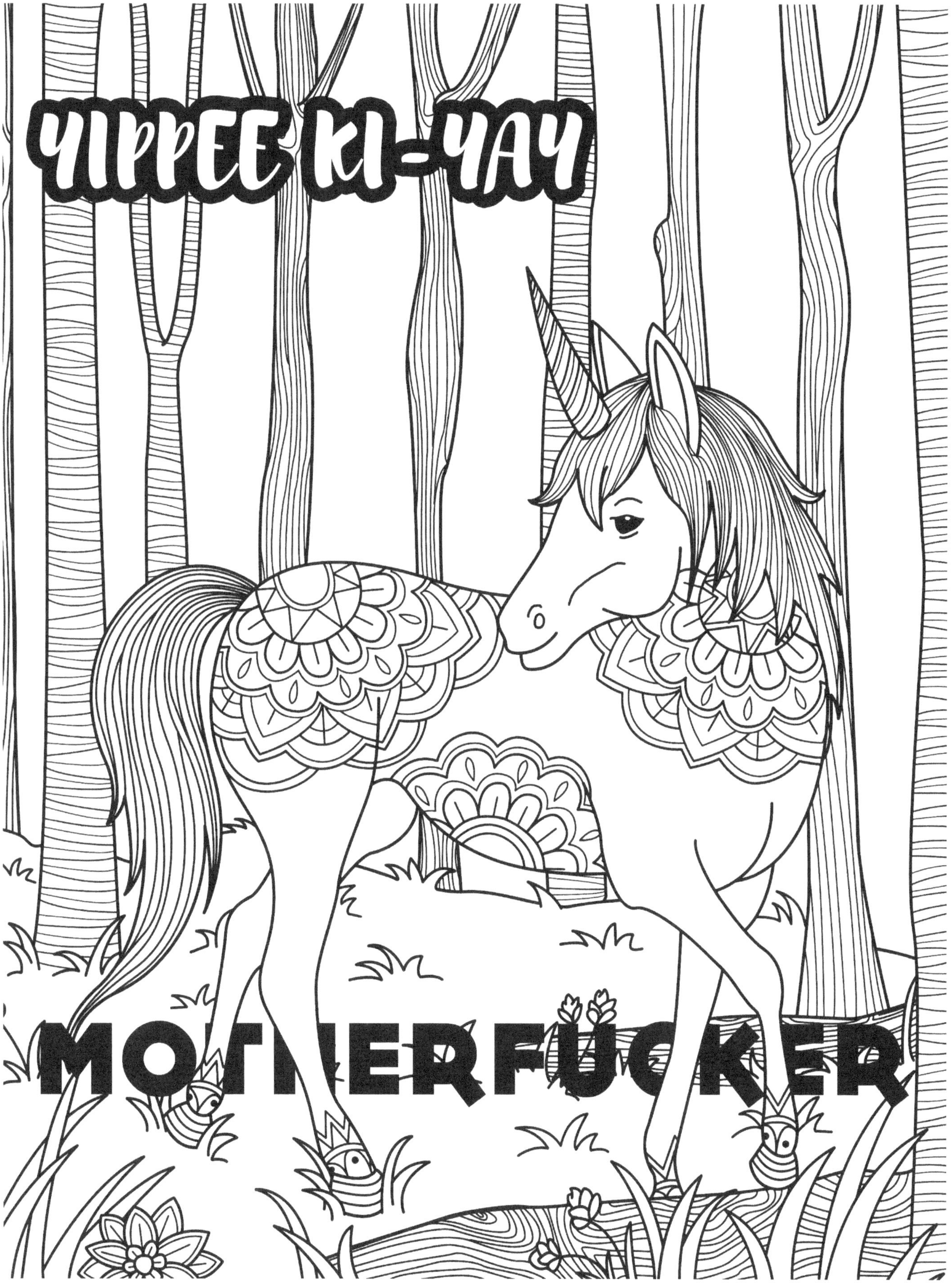
YIPPEE KI-YAY
MOTHERFUCKER

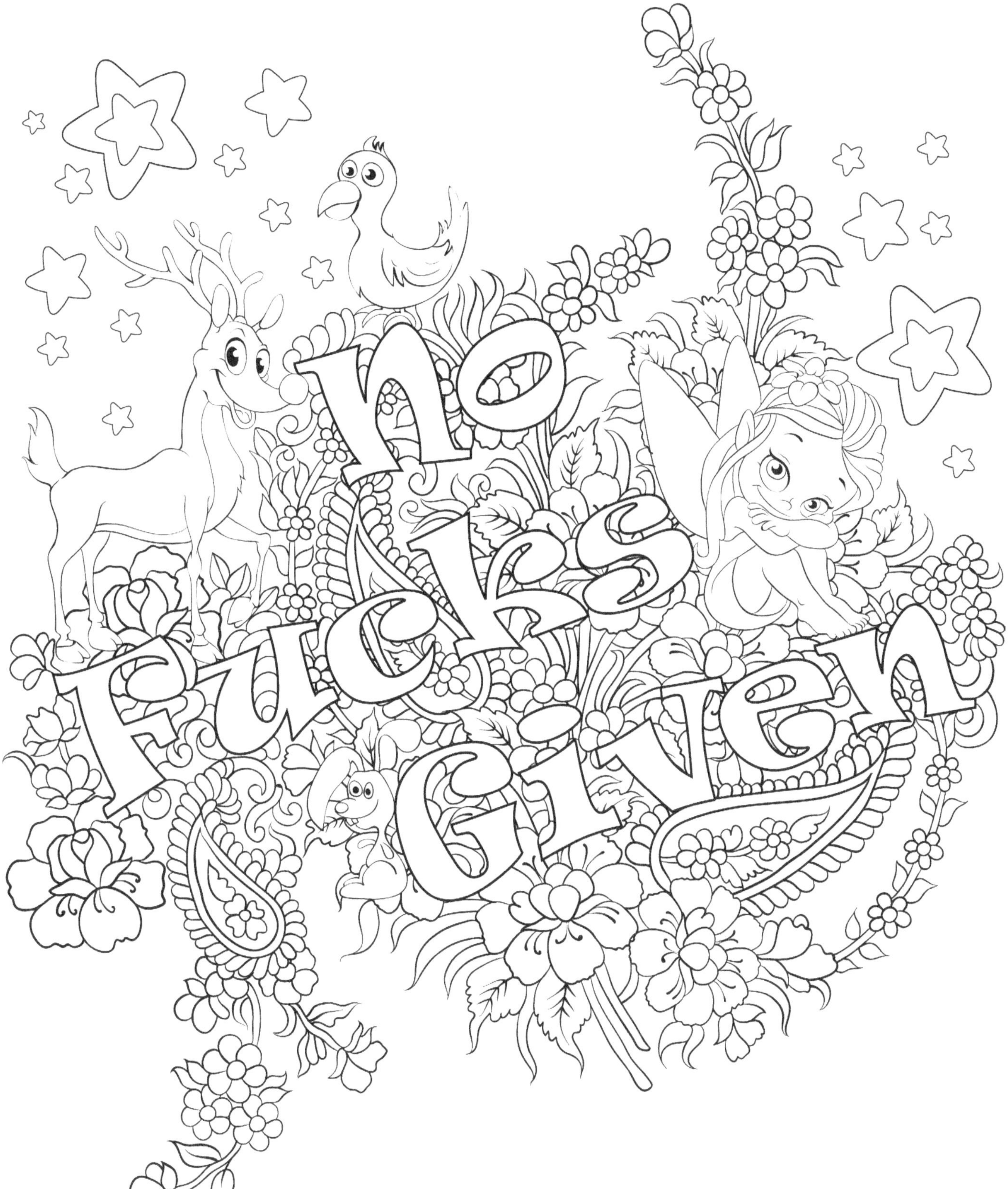
no Fucks Given

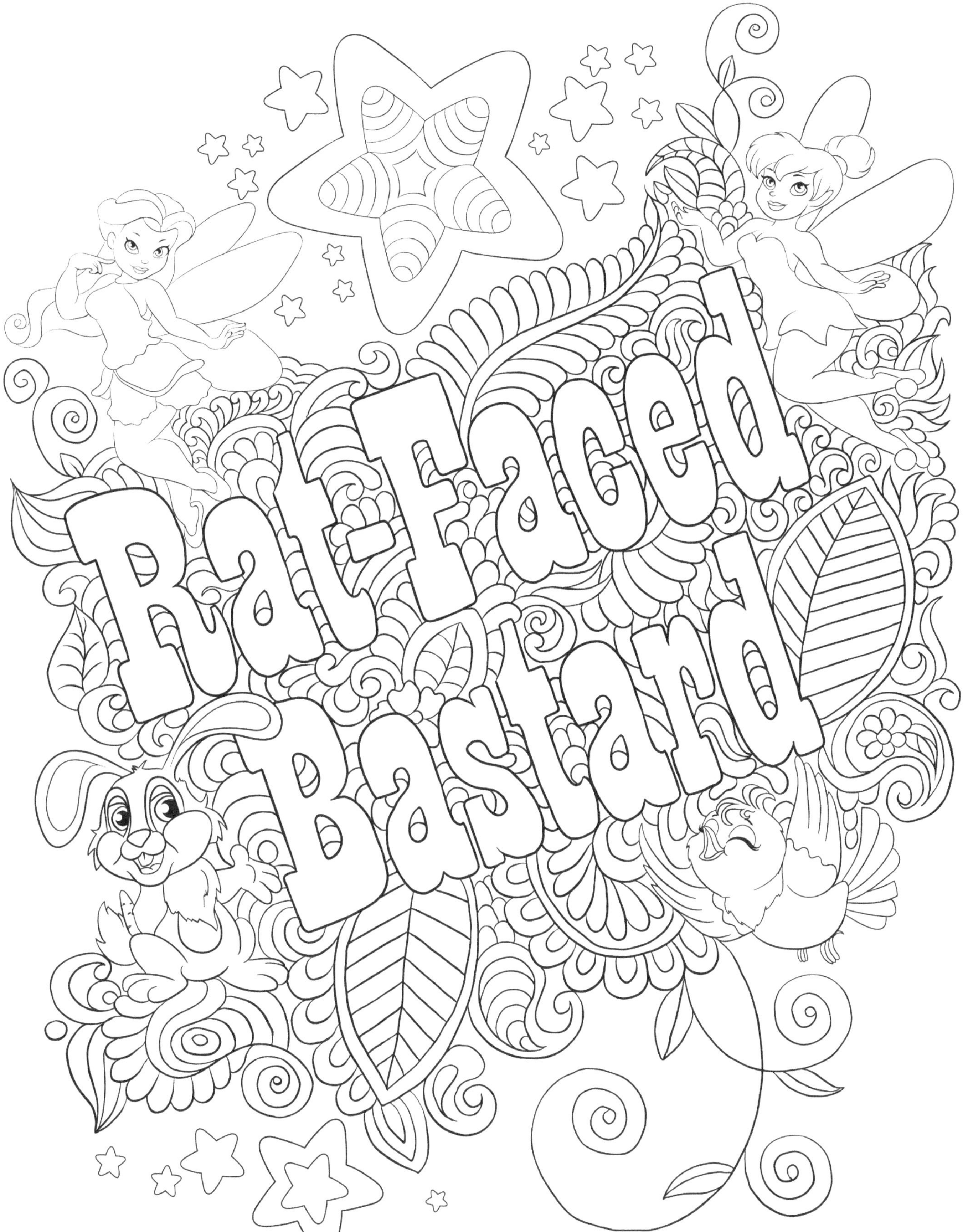
Rat-Faced
Bastard

www.ingramcontent.com/pod-product-compliance
Lightning Source LLC
Chambersburg PA
CBHW080640190526
45169CB00009B/3447
9781530976973